Keyboarding for the Christian School

Keyboarding for the Christian School

Leanne Beitel

iUniverse, Inc.
New York Lincoln Shanghai

Keyboarding for the Christian School

iUniverse books may be ordered through booksellers or by contacting:

iUniverse
2021 Pine Lake Road, Suite 100
Lincoln, NE 68512
www.iuniverse.com
1-800-Authors (1-800-288-4677)

ISBN-13: 978-0-595-38319-1 (pbk)
ISBN-13: 978-0-595-82691-9 (ebk)
ISBN-10: 0-595-38319-X (pbk)
ISBN-10: 0-595-82691-1 (ebk)

Printed in the United States of America

This textbook is dedicated to the keyboarding students (and parents) at Calvary Christian Academy who encouraged, and faithfully edited and tested this material; to Ms. Sue Tidwell for her encouragement and support, to the staff (including Mrs. Patsy Bautista and Mr. Bradley Moore) for their their prayers and love and devotion to Jesus Christ, my family; to my husband, Curtis for his tremendous understanding and love; and above all to my LORD and King. Thank you!

Table of Contents

Introduction

This book uses 12-point Times New Roman font for each exercise; which is the default of most word processors. Each lesson is intentionally brief to allow for shorter class time, review, or to complete more than one lesson at a time or to supplement another curriculum. If the instructor desires, each exercise may be repeated for further key memorization.

Touch Typing Technique

In order to reach all of the keys easily and to type efficiently, there are certain techniques to use.

1. Sit up straight and lean in at the waist.
2. Keep feet flat on the floor (with one slightly in front of the other for balance).
3. Body is one hand-span (or length) from the keyboard.
4. The J key on the keyboard is opposite of your bellybutton.
5. Hands are on the homerow (to be introduced in the first lesson)
6. Curve fingers.
7. Elbows are naturally at your side.
8. Wrists are level (not touching the table or the keyboard).
9. Eyes are looking at the copy.
10. Keyboard is parallel to the table.

11. The text or copy is placed on the right-hand side.

12. Use quick, snappy strokes in a rhythmic pace.

Lesson 1: F and J Keys

*Please notice that each exercise line does not end at the same place. This is due to character spacing. Each letter, number, symbol, etc. is considered a character. Each character takes up so much space on a page. The **i** takes up less space than an **m**. This book also uses two spaces after each period ending a sentence.*

The homerow keys are: **A S D F J K L ;**

Place your left pinky on the **A**. Allow the other fingers to rest on the **S**, **D**, and **F** keys. Both thumbs will hover over the space bar. Place your right index finger on the J. Allow the other fingers to rest on the **K**, **L**, and ; keys. Most typists use their right thumb to press the space bar.

A. *Type the **f** in sets of three 10 times as shown below:*

fff fff fff fff fff fff fff fff fff fff

B. *Type the **j** in sets of three 10 times as shown below:*

jjj jjj jjj jjj jjj jjj jjj jjj jjj jjj

C. *Type the **f** and **j** in sets of three 10 times as shown below:*

fff jjj fff jjj ffj jjf fjf jfj fff jjj

D. *Type the **f** and **j** in sets of three 10 times pressing **Enter** with your right pinky at the end of each line as shown below:*

fff jjj fff jjj fff jjj fff jjj fff jjj
jjj fff jjj fff jjj fff jjj fff jjj fff
fjf fjf fjf jfj jfj ffj jjf ffj jjf fjf

Lesson 2: D and K Keys

*Use your left middle finger for typing the **D**. Use your right middle finger for typing the **K**.*

A. *Type the **d** in sets of three 10 times as shown below:*

ddd ddd ddd ddd ddd ddd ddd ddd ddd ddd

B. *Type the **k** in sets of three 10 times as shown below:*

kkk kkk kkk kkk kkk kkk kkk kkk kkk kkk

C. *Type the **d** and **k** in sets of three 10 times as shown below:*

ddd kkk ddd kkk ddk kkd dkd kdk ddd kkk

D. *Type the **d** and **k** in sets of three 10 times pressing **Enter** with your right pinky at the end of each line as shown below:*

ddd kkk ddd kkk ddd kkk ddd kkk ddd kkk
kkk ddd kkk ddd kkk ddd kkk ddd kkk ddd
dkd dkd dkd kdk kdk ddk kkd ddk kkd dkd

E. *Practice the new keys with the previous lesson. Type each line two times each. Press **Enter** once after each line. Press **Enter** twice after each set of two lines. This will leave one blank line after each set.*

fff fff fff fff fff jjj jjj jjj jjj jjj
ddd ddd ddd ddd ddd kkk kkk kkk kkk kkk
fjf fjf jfj jfj dkd dkd kdk kdk fdf fdf
jkj jkj fkd fkd fjf fjf kjd kjd kfd kfd
jkf jkf dfk dfk ffk ffk jjk jjk jjd jjd

Lesson 3:   S and L Keys

*Use your left ring finger for typing the **S**. Use your right ring finger for typing the **L**.*

A. *Type the **s** in sets of three 10 times as shown below:*

sss sss sss sss sss sss sss sss sss sss

B. *Type the **l** in sets of three 10 times as shown below:*

lll lll lll lll lll lll lll lll lll lll

C. *Type the **s** and **l** in sets of three 10 times as shown below:*

sss lll sss lll ssl sls lsl sss lll

D. *Type the **s** and **l** in sets of three 10 times pressing **Enter** with your right pinky at the end of each line as shown below:*

sss lll sss lll sss lll sss lll sss lll
lll sss lll sss lll sss lll sss lll sss
sls sls sls lsl lsl ssl ssl ssl lls sll

E. *Practice the new keys with the previous lessons. Type each line two times each. Press **Enter** once after each line. Press **Enter** twice after each set of two lines. This will leave one blank line after each set.*

ddd ddd ddd ddd ddd kkk kkk kkk kkk kkk
sss sss sss sss sss lll lll lll lll lll
fjf fjf jfj jfj dkd dkd kdk kdk fdf fdf
fsl fsl jks jks lks lks kjs kjs fks fks
jls jls kls kls fsk fsk skl skl dsl dsl

Lesson 4: A and ; Keys

Use your left pinky finger for typing the A. Use your right pinky finger for typing the ;.

A. *Type the **a** in sets of three 10 times as shown below:*

aaa aaa aaa aaa aaa aaa aaa aaa aaa aaa

B. *Type the **;** in sets of three 10 times as shown below:*

;;; ;;; ;;; ;;; ;;; ;;; ;;; ;;; ;;; ;;;

C. *Type the **a** and **;** in sets of three 10 times as shown below:*

aaa ;;; aaa ;;; aa; ;;a a;a ;a; aaa ;;;

D. *Type the **a** and **;** in sets of three 10 times pressing **Enter** with your right pinky at the end of each line as shown below:*

aaa ;;; aaa ;;; aaa ;;; aaa ;;; aaa ;;;
;;; aaa ;;; aaa ;;; aaa ;;; aaa ;;; aaa
a;a a;a a;a ;a; ;a; aa; ;;a aa; ;;a a;a

E. *Practice the new keys with the previous lessons. Type each line two times each. Press **Enter** once after each line. Press **Enter** twice after each set of two lines. This will leave one blank line after each set.*

fff fff fff fff fff jjj jjj jjj jjj jjj
ddd ddd ddd ddd ddd kkk kkk kkk kkk kkk
sss sss sss sss sss lll lll lll lll lll
aaa aaa aaa aaa aaa ;;; ;;; ;;; ;;; ;;;
asd asd ;lk ;lk kla kla fla fla jds jds

Lesson 5: G and H Keys

*Use your left index finger (F) for typing the **G**. Use your right index finger (J) for typing the **H**.*

A. *Type the **g** in sets of three 10 times as shown below:*

ggg ggg ggg ggg ggg ggg ggg ggg ggg ggg

B. *Type the **h** in sets of three 10 times as shown below:*

hhh hhh hhh hhh hhh hhh hhh hhh hhh hhh

C. *Type the **g** and **h** in sets of three 10 times as shown below:*

ggg hhh ggg hhh ggg hhh ggg hhh ggg hhh

D. *Type the **g** and **h** in sets of three 10 times pressing **Enter** with your right pinky at the end of each line as shown below:*

ggg hhh ggg hhh ggg hhh ggg hhh ggg hhh
hhh ggg hhh ggg hhh ggg hhh ggg hhh ggg
ghg ghg hgh hgh ggh ggh hhg hhg ggh hhg

E. *Practice the new keys with the previous lessons. Type each line two times each. Press **Enter** once after each line. Press **Enter** twice after each set of two lines. This will leave one blank line after each set.*

ddd ddd ddd ddd ddd kkk kkk kkk kkk kkk
sss sss sss sss sss lll lll lll lll lll
aaa aaa aaa aaa aaa ;;; ;;; ;;; ;;; ;;;
ggg ggg ggg ggg ggg hhh hhh hhh hhh hhh
fgf gfg jhj ksj las jks ;aj ;hg dlh sjg

Lesson 6: Review

A. Type the keys learned in sets of three as shown below:

fff jjj fff jjj fff jjj fff jjj fff jjj

ddd kkk ddd kkk ddd kkk ddd kkk ddd kkk

sss lll sss lll sss lll sss lll sss lll

aaa ;;; aaa ;;; aaa ;;; aaa ;;; aaa ;;;

ggg hhh ggg hhh ggg hhh ggg hhh ggg hhh

B. Type the f and j in sets of three 10 times as shown below:

fff fff fff fff fff fff fff fff fff fff

jjj jjj jjj jjj jjj jjj jjj jjj jjj jjj

C. Type the d and k in sets of three 10 times as shown below:

ddd ddd ddd ddd ddd ddd ddd ddd ddd ddd

kkk kkk kkk kkk kkk kkk kkk kkk kkk kkk

D. Type the s and l in sets of three 10 times as shown below:

sss sss sss sss sss sss sss sss sss sss

lll lll lll lll lll lll lll lll lll lll

E. Type the a and ; in sets of three 10 times as shown below:

aaa aaa aaa aaa aaa aaa aaa aaa aaa aaa

;;; ;;; ;;; ;;; ;;; ;;; ;;; ;;; ;;; ;;;

F. Type the g and h in sets of three 10 times as shown below:

ggg ggg ggg ggg ggg ggg ggg ggg ggg ggg

hhh hhh hhh hhh hhh hhh hhh hhh hhh hhh

*G. Practice the short words. Type each line once. Press **Enter** once after each line.*

sad sad sad sad sad sad sad sad sad sad

lash lash lash lash lash lash lash lash lash lash

salad salad salad salad salad salad salad salad salad salad

Lesson 7: E and I Keys

*Use your left middle finger (D) for typing the **E**. Use your right middle finger (K) for typing the **I**.*

A. *Type the **e** in sets of three 10 times as shown below:*

eee eee eee eee eee eee eee eee eee eee

B. *Type the **i** in sets of three 10 times as shown below:*

iii iii iii iii iii iii iii iii iii iii

C. *Type the **e** and **i** in sets of three 10 times as shown below:*

eee iii eee iii eee iii eee iii eee iii

D. *Type the **e** and **i** in sets of three 10 times pressing **Enter** with your right pinky at the end of each line as shown below:*

eee iii eee iii eee iii eee iii eee iii
iii eee iii eee iii eee iii eee iii eee
eie iei eei iie eie eii iee eie iei iee

E. *Practice the new keys with the previous keys learned. Type each line two times each. Press **Enter** once after each line. Press **Enter** twice after each set of two lines. This will leave one blank line after each set.*

aaa aaa aaa aaa aaa ;;; ;;; ;;; ;;; ;;;
ggg ggg ggg ggg ggg hhh hhh hhh hhh hhh
eee eee eee eee eee iii iii iii iii iii
sad fad lad dad lid fed fig said feel deal

Lesson 8:   R and U Keys

Use your left index finger (F) for typing the **R**. *Use your right index finger (J) for typing the* **U**.

A. *Type the* **r** *in sets of three 10 times as shown below:*

rrr rrr rrr rrr rrr rrr rrr rrr rrr rrr

B. *Type the* **u** *in sets of three 10 times as shown below:*

uuu uuu uuu uuu uuu uuu uuu uuu uuu uuu

C. *Type the* **r** *and* **u** *in sets of three 10 times as shown below:*

rrr uuu rrr uuu rrr uuu rrr uuu rrr uuu

D. *Type the* **r** *and* **u** *in sets of three 10 times pressing* **Enter** *with your right pinky at the end of each line as shown below:*

rrr uuu rrr uuu rrr uuu rrr uuu rrr uuu
uuu rrr uuu rrr uuu rrr uuu rrr uuu rrr
rur uru rru uur ruu uur rur uru ruu urr

E. *Practice the new keys with the previous keys learned. Type each line two times each. Press* **Enter** *once after each line. Press* **Enter** *twice after each set of two lines. This will leave one blank line after each set.*

aaa aaa aaa aaa aaa ;;; ;;; ;;; ;;; ;;;
ggg ggg ggg ggg ggg hhh hhh hhh hhh hhh
eee eee eee eee eee iii iii iii iii iii
rrr rrr rrr rrr rrr uuu uuu uuu uuu uuu
flag dish heal fuss grill fear deal flask salad frills

Lesson 9: W and O Keys

*Use your left ring finger (S) for typing the **W**. Use your right ring finger (L) for typing the **O**.*

*A. Type the **w** in sets of three 10 times as shown below:*

www www www www www www www www www www

*B. Type the **o** in sets of three 10 times as shown below:*

ooo ooo ooo ooo ooo ooo ooo ooo ooo ooo

*C. Type the **w** and **o** in sets of three 10 times as shown below:*

www ooo www ooo www ooo www ooo www ooo

*D. Type the **w** and **o** in sets of three 10 times pressing **Enter** with your right pinky at the end of each line as shown below:*

www ooo www ooo www ooo www ooo www ooo
ooo www ooo www ooo www ooo www ooo www
wwo oow wow woo owo oow www ooo wow oow

*E. Practice the new keys with the previous keys learned. Type each line two times each. Press **Enter** once after each line. Press **Enter** twice after each set of two lines. This will leave one blank line after each set.*

ggg ggg ggg ggg ggg hhh hhh hhh hhh hhh
eee eee eee eee eee iii iii iii iii iii
rrr rrr rrr rrr rrr uuu uuu uuu uuu uuu
www www www www www ooo ooo ooo ooo ooo
row fowl hurl fare loud road load grade sore drawer

Lesson 10: T and Y Keys

*Use your left index finger (F) for typing the **T**. Use your right index finger (J) for typing the **Y**.*

A. *Type the **t** in sets of three 10 times as shown below:*

ttt ttt ttt ttt ttt ttt ttt ttt ttt ttt

B. *Type the **y** in sets of three 10 times as shown below:*

yyy yyy yyy yyy yyy yyy yyy yyy yyy yyy

C. *Type the **t** and **y** in sets of three 10 times as shown below:*

ttt yyy ttt yyy ttt yyy ttt yyy ttt yyy

D. *Type the **t** and **y** in sets of three 10 times pressing **Enter** with your right pinky at the end of each line as shown below:*

ttt yyy ttt yyy ttt yyy ttt yyy ttt yyy
yyy ttt yyy ttt yyy ttt yyy ttt yyy ttt
tyt yty tty yyt yty tyt yyt tty tyt yty

E. *Practice the new keys with the previous keys learned. Type each line two times each. Press **Enter** once after each line. Press **Enter** twice after each set of two lines. This will leave one blank line after each set.*

eee eee eee eee eee iii iii iii iii iii
rrr rrr rrr rrr rrr uuu uuu uuu uuu uuu
www www www www www ooo ooo ooo ooo ooo
ttt ttt ttt ttt ttt yyy yyy yyy yyy yyy
for oil two your good life howl trade grate safely

Lesson 11:   Q and P Keys

Use your left pinky finger (A) for typing the **Q**. *Use your right pinky finger (;) for typing the* **P**.

A. *Type the* **q** *in sets of three 10 times as shown below:*

qqq qqq qqq qqq qqq qqq qqq qqq qqq qqq

B. *Type the* **p** *in sets of three 10 times as shown below:*

ppp ppp ppp ppp ppp ppp ppp ppp ppp ppp

C. *Type the* **q** *and* **p** *in sets of three 10 times as shown below:*

qqq ppp qqq ppp qqq ppp qqq ppp qqq ppp

D. *Type the* **q** *and* **p** *in sets of three 10 times pressing* **Enter** *with your right pinky at the end of each line as shown below:*

qqq ppp qqq ppp qqq ppp qqq ppp qqq ppp
ppp qqq ppp qqq ppp qqq ppp qqq ppp qqq
qpq pqp qqp ppq qpq pqp qqp ppq qpp pqq

E. *Practice the new keys with the previous keys learned. Type each line two times each. Press* **Enter** *once after each line. Press* **Enter** *twice after each set of two lines. This will leave one blank line after each set.*

rrr rrr rrr rrr rrr uuu uuu uuu uuu uuu

www www www www www ooo ooo ooo ooo ooo

ttt ttt ttt ttt ttt yyy yyy yyy yyy yyy

qqq qqq qqq qqq qqq ppp ppp ppp ppp ppp

page trap prod gate trait hope wood proud quip quid

Lesson 12: Review

A. Type the keys learned in sets of three as shown below:

eee iii eee iii eee iii eee iii eee iii

rrr uuu rrr uuu rrr uuu rrr uuu rrr uuu

www ooo www ooo www ooo www ooo www ooo

ttt yyy ttt yyy ttt yyy ttt yyy ttt yyy

qqq ppp qqq ppp qqq ppp qqq ppp qqq ppp

B. Type the e and i in sets of three 10 times as shown below:

eee eee eee eee eee eee eee eee eee eee

iii iii iii iii iii iii iii iii iii iii

C. Type the r and u in sets of three 10 times as shown below:

rrr rrr rrr rrr rrr rrr rrr rrr rrr rrr

uuu uuu uuu uuu uuu uuu uuu uuu uuu uuu

D. Type the w and o in sets of three 10 times as shown below:

www www www www www www www www www www

ooo ooo ooo ooo ooo ooo ooo ooo ooo ooo

E. Type the t and y in sets of three 10 times as shown below:

ttt ttt ttt ttt ttt ttt ttt ttt ttt ttt

yyy yyy yyy yyy yyy yyy yyy yyy yyy yyy

F. Type the q and p in sets of three 10 times as shown below:

qqq qqq qqq qqq qqq qqq qqq qqq qqq qqq

ppp ppp ppp ppp ppp ppp ppp ppp ppp ppp

*G. Practice the short words. Type each line once. Press **Enter** once after each line.*

guide guide guide guide guide guide guide guide guide guide

equip equip equip equip equip equip equip equip equip equip

yoke yoke yoke yoke yoke yoke yoke yoke yoke yoke

Lesson 13:   B and N Keys

*Use your left index finger (F) for typing the **B**. Use your right index finger (J) for typing the **N**. The lower row keys are harder to reach unless you curve your fingers. Since your left index finger is stronger than the right, you have more keys to reach.*

A. *Type the **b** in sets of three 10 times as shown below:*

bbb bbb bbb bbb bbb bbb bbb bbb bbb bbb

B. *Type the **n** in sets of three 10 times as shown below:*

nnn nnn nnn nnn nnn nnn nnn nnn nnn nnn

C. *Type the **b** and **n** in sets of three 10 times as shown below:*

bbb nnn bbb nnn bbb nnn bbb nnn bbb nnn

D. *Type the **b** and **n** in sets of three 10 times pressing **Enter** with your right pinky at the end of each line as shown below:*

bbb nnn bbb nnn bbb nnn bbb nnn bbb nnn
nnn bbb nnn bbb nnn bbb nnn bbb nnn bbb
bnb nbn bbn nnb bnn nbb bnb nbn bbn nnb

E. *Practice the new keys with the previous keys learned. Type each line two times each. Press **Enter** once after each line. Press **Enter** twice after each set of two lines. This will leave one blank line after each set.*

www www www www www ooo ooo ooo ooo ooo
ttt ttt ttt ttt ttt yyy yyy yyy yyy yyy
qqq qqq qqq qqq qqq ppp ppp ppp ppp ppp
bbb bbb bbb bbb bbb nnn nnn nnn nnn nnn
knoll group saber grift dwarf plane train seen lobe berry

Lesson 14: V and M Keys

Use your left index finger (F) for typing the V. Use your right index finger (J) for typing the M.

A. *Type the **v** in sets of three 10 times as shown below:*

vvv vvv vvv vvv vvv vvv vvv vvv vvv vvv

B. *Type the **m** in sets of three 10 times as shown below:*

mmm mmm mmm mmm mmm mmm mmm mmm mmm mmm

C. *Type the **v** and **m** in sets of three 10 times as shown below:*

vvv mmm vvv mmm vvv mmm vvv mmm vvv mmm

D. *Type the **v** and **m** in sets of three 10 times pressing **Enter** with your right pinky at the end of each line as shown below:*

vvv mmm vvv mmm vvv mmm vvv mmm vvv mmm
mmm vvv mmm vvv mmm vvv mmm vvv mmm vvv
mvm vmv vvm mmv vvm mmv vmv mvm mmv vvm

E. *Practice the new keys with the previous keys learned. Type each line two times each. Press **Enter** once after each line. Press **Enter** twice after each set of two lines. This will leave one blank line after each set.*

ttt ttt ttt ttt ttt yyy yyy yyy yyy yyy
qqq qqq qqq qqq qqq ppp ppp ppp ppp ppp
bbb bbb bbb bbb bbb nnn nnn nnn nnn nnn
vvv vvv vvv vvv vvv mmm mmm mmm mmm mmm
groom drove snail flavor loom noon broom favor groove savor

Lesson 15:   C and , Keys

*Use your left middle finger (D) for typing the **C**. Use your right middle finger (K) for typing the ,. Use one space after a comma. There are no spaces before the comma.*

A. *Type the **c** in sets of three 10 times as shown below:*

ccc ccc ccc ccc ccc ccc ccc ccc ccc ccc

B. *Type the , in sets of three 10 times as shown below:*

,,, ,,, ,,, ,,, ,,, ,,, ,,, ,,, ,,, ,,,

C. *Type the **c** and, in sets of three 10 times as shown below:*

ccc ,,, ccc ,,, ccc ,,, ccc ,,, ccc ,,,

D. *Type the **c** and, in sets of three 10 times pressing **Enter** with your right pinky at the end of each line as shown below:*

ccc ,,, ccc ,,, ccc ,,, ccc ,,, ccc ,,,
,,, ccc ,,, ccc ,,, ccc ,,, ccc ,,, ccc
c,c ,c, cc, ,,c c,c ,c, cc, ,,c c,c ,c,

E. *Practice the new keys with the previous keys learned. Type each line two times each. Press **Enter** once after each line. Press **Enter** twice after each set of two lines. This will leave one blank line after each set.*

qqq qqq qqq qqq qqq ppp ppp ppp ppp ppp
bbb bbb bbb bbb bbb nnn nnn nnn nnn nnn
vvv vvv vvv vvv vvv mmm mmm mmm mmm mmm
ccc ccc ccc ccc ccc ,,, ,,, ,,, ,,, ,,,
call, mine, voice, crate, blame, crane, small, name, clams, neighbor,

Lesson 16: X and . Keys

*Use your left ring finger (S) for typing the **X**. Use your right ring finger (L) for typing the **.**. Use two spaces after a period. There are no spaces before the period.*

A. *Type the **x** in sets of three 10 times as shown below:*

xxx xxx xxx xxx xxx xxx xxx xxx xxx xxx

B. *Type the **.** in sets of three 10 times as shown below:*

... ...

C. *Type the **x** and **.** in sets of three 10 times as shown below:*

xxx ... xxx ... xxx ... xxx ... xxx ...

D. *Type the **x** and **.** in sets of three 10 times pressing **Enter** with your right pinky at the end of each line as shown below:*

xxx ... xxx ... xxx ... xxx ... xxx ...
... xxx ... xxx ... xxx ... xxx ... xxx
x.x .x. xx. ..x x.x .x. xx. ..x x.x .x.

E. *Practice the new keys with the previous keys learned. Type each line two times each. Press **Enter** once after each line. Press **Enter** twice after each set of two lines. This will leave one blank line after each set.*

qqq qqq qqq qqq qqq ppp ppp ppp ppp ppp
bbb bbb bbb bbb bbb nnn nnn nnn nnn nnn

vvv vvv vvv vvv vvv mmm mmm mmm mmm mmm
ccc ccc ccc ccc ccc ,,, ,,, ,,, ,,, ,,,

exam. exact. extra. oxcart. oxen. extract. examine. exactly. extraneous. xylophone.

Lesson 17: Z and / Keys

*Use your left pinky finger (A) for typing the **Z**. Use your right pinky finger (;) for typing the /. There are no spaces before or after the slash (also known as the forward slash) (/).*

A. *Type the z in sets of three 10 times as shown below:*

zzz zzz zzz zzz zzz zzz zzz zzz zzz zzz

B. *Type the/in sets of three 10 times as shown below:*

/// /// /// /// /// /// /// /// /// ///

C. *Type the z and/in sets of three 10 times as shown below:*

zzz /// zzz /// zzz /// zzz /// zzz ///

D. *Type the z and / in sets of three 10 times pressing **Enter** with your right pinky at the end of each line as shown below:*

zzz /// zzz /// zzz /// zzz /// zzz ///
/// zzz /// zzz /// zzz /// zzz /// zzz
z/z /z/ zz/ //z z/z /z/ zz/ //z z/z /z/

E. *Practice the new keys with the previous keys learned. Type each line two times each. Press **Enter** once after each line. Press **Enter** twice after each set of two lines. This will leave one blank line after each set.*

bbb bbb bbb bbb bbb nnn nnn nnn nnn nnn

vvv vvv vvv vvv vvv mmm mmm mmm mmm mmm

ccc ccc ccc ccc ccc ,,, ,,, ,,, ,,, ,,,

xxx xxx xxx xxx xxx ... ...

zebra zeal zealot zero he/she cats/dogs hide/seek start/stop input/output stop/go

Lesson 18: Shift Keys

*Use your left pinky finger (A) for typing the **left shift key**. Use your right pinky finger (;) for typing the **right shift key**. You use the left shift key for typing characters on the right side. You use the right shift key for typing characters on the left side. Hold down the shift key while pressing the character. The shift key is used to capitalize letters or to use the top displayed character on each key.*

A. *Type the **sentence** two times:*

This is the day that the Lord has made. Let us rejoice and be glad in it.

B. *Type the **sentence** two times:*

Choose My instruction instead of silver, knowledge rather than choice gold, for wisdom is more precious than rubies, and nothing you desire can compare with her.

C. *Type the **sentence** two times:*

So is My Word that goes out from My mouth: It will not return to Me empty, but will accomplish what I desire and achieve the purpose for which I sent it.

D. *Practice the new keys with the previous keys learned. Type each line two times each. Press **Enter** once after each line. Press **Enter** twice after each set of two lines. This will leave one blank line after each set.*

vvv vvv vvv vvv vvv mmm mmm mmm mmm mmm

ccc ccc ccc ccc ccc ,,, ,,, ,,, ,,, ,,,

xxx xxx xxx xxx xxx ... ...

zzz zzz zzz zzz zzz /// /// /// /// ///

With the tongue we praise our Lord and Father, and with it we curse men, who have been made in the likeness of God.

Lesson 19: : and ? Keys

*Use your right pinky finger (;) for typing the **colon** (:). Use your right pinky finger (;) for typing the **question mark** (?). You use the left shift key for typing the colon and question mark. There is no space before the colon, but two spaces after it unless it is used in time notation such as 3:30 p.m. The question mark also has no space before it but two spaces after it.*

A. *Type the **sentence** two times:*

What is impossible with men is possible with God.

B. *Type the **sentence** two times:*

One thing I ask of the LORD, this is what I seek: that I may dwell in the house of the LORD all the days of my life, to gaze upon the beauty of the LORD and to seek Him in His temple.

C. *Type the **sentence** two times:*

How can you believe if you accept praise from one another, yet make no effort to obtain the praise that comes from the only God?

D. *Practice the new keys with the previous keys learned. Type each line two times each. Press **Enter** once after each line. Press **Enter** twice after each set of two lines. This will leave one blank line after each set.*

vvv vvv vvv vvv vvv mmm mmm mmm mmm mmm

ccc ccc ccc ccc ccc ,,, ,,, ,,, ,,, ,,,

xxx xxx xxx xxx xxx ... ...

zzz zzz zzz zzz zzz /// /// /// /// ////

::: ::: ::: ??? ??? ??? ::? ??: :?: ?:?

Lesson 20: ' and " Keys

*Use your right pinky finger (;) for typing the **apostrophe** ('). Use your right pinky finger (;) for typing the **quotation mark** ("). You use the left shift key for typing the apostrophe and quotation mark.*

A. *Type the **sentence** two times:*

Do not be misled: "Bad company corrupts good character."

B. *Type the **sentence** two times:*

"But I say unto you, that every idle word that men shall speak, they shall give account thereof in the Day of Judgment."

C. *Type the **sentence** two times:*

"For we are God's workmanship, created in Christ Jesus to do good works, which God prepared in advance for us to do."

D. *Practice the previous keys learned. Type each line two times each. Press **Enter** once after each line. Press **Enter** twice after each set of two lines. This will leave one blank line after each set.*

vvv vvv vvv vvv vvv mmm mmm mmm mmm mmm

ccc ccc ccc ccc ccc ,,, ,,, ,,, ,,, ,,,

xxx xxx xxx xxx xxx … … … … …

zzz zzz zzz zzz zzz /// /// /// /// ///

Lesson 21:   Numbers and Symbols: 1/! and 0/) Keys

[Matthew 10:30, "And even the very hairs of your head are all numbered."]

*Use your left pinky finger (A) for typing the **one (1)** and **exclamation point (!)**. Use your right pinky finger (;) for typing the **zero (0)** and **closed/ending parenthesis)**. You use the right shift key for typing the exclamation point and the left shift key for typing the closed/ending parenthesis.*

A. *Type the **1** in sets of three 10 times as shown below:*

111 111 111 111 111 111 111 111 111 111

B. *Type the **0** in sets of three 10 times as shown below:*

000 000 000 000 000 000 000 000 000 000

C. *Type the **1** and **0** in sets of three 10 times as shown below:*

111 000 111 000 110 001 110 001 010 101

D. *Type the **!** in sets of three 10 times as shown below:*

!!! !!! !!! !!! !!! !!! !!! !!! !!! !!!

E. *Type the **)** in sets of three 10 times as shown below:*

))))))))))))))))))))))))))))))

F. *Type the **!** and **)** in sets of three 10 times as shown below:*

!!!))) !!!))) !!)))! !)! !!) !!)))!

Lesson 22: Numbers and Symbols: 2/@ and 9/(Keys

[Matthew 10:30, "And even the very hairs of your head are all numbered."]

*Use your left ring finger (S) for typing the **two (2)** and **at symbol (@)**. Use your right ring finger (L) for typing the **nine (9)** and **open parenthesis (**. You use the right shift key for typing the at symbol and the left shift key for typing the closed/ending parenthesis.*

A. *Type the **2** in sets of three 10 times as shown below:*

222 222 222 222 222 222 222 222 222 222

B. *Type the **9** in sets of three 10 times as shown below:*

999 999 999 999 999 999 999 999 999 999

C. *Type the **2** and **9** in sets of three 10 times as shown below:*

222 999 229 992 292 929 229 992 222 999

D. *Type the **@** in sets of three 10 times as shown below:*

@@@ @@@ @@@ @@@ @@@ @@@ @@@ @@@ @@@ @@@

E. *Type the **(** in sets of three 10 times as shown below:*

((((((((((((((((((((((((((((((

F. *Type the **@** and **(** in sets of three 10 times as shown below:*

@@@ (((@(@ (@(@@(((@ @@(((@ @@@ (((

Lesson 23:   Numbers and Symbols: 3/# and 8/* Keys

[Matthew 10:30, "And even the very hairs of your head are all numbered."]

*Use your left middle finger (D) for typing the **three (3)** and **pound symbol (#)**. Use your right middle finger (K) for typing the **eight (8)** and **asterisk (*)**. You use the right shift key for typing the pound symbol and the left shift key for typing the asterisk.*

A. *Type the 3 in sets of three 10 times as shown below:*

333 333 333 333 333 333 333 333 333 333

B. *Type the 8 in sets of three 10 times as shown below:*

888 888 888 888 888 888 888 888 888 888

C. *Type the 3 and 8 in sets of three 10 times as shown below:*

333 888 338 883 383 838 388 883 333 888

D. *Type the # in sets of three 10 times as shown below:*

###

E. *Type the * in sets of three 10 times as shown below:*

*** *** *** *** *** *** *** *** *** ***

F. *Type the # and * in sets of three 10 times as shown below:*

*** ##* **# #*# *#* ##* **# ### ***

Lesson 24: Numbers and Symbols: 4/$ and 7/& Keys

[Matthew 10:30, "And even the very hairs of your head are all numbered."]

*Use your left index finger (F) for typing the **four (4)** and **dollar sign ($)**. Use your right index finger (J) for typing the **seven (7)** and **ampersand (&)**. You use the right shift key for typing the dollar sign and the left shift key for typing the ampersand.*

A. *Type the **4** in sets of three 10 times as shown below:*

444 444 444 444 444 444 444 444 444 444

B. *Type the **7** in sets of three 10 times as shown below:*

777 777 777 777 777 777 777 777 777 777

C. *Type the **4** and **7** in sets of three 10 times as shown below:*

444 777 447 774 474 747 477 774 444 777

D. *Type the **$** in sets of three 10 times as shown below:*

$$$ $$$ $$$ $$$ $$$ $$$ $$$ $$$ $$$ $$$

E. *Type the **&** in sets of three 10 times as shown below:*

&&& &&& &&& &&& &&& &&& &&& &&& &&& &&&

F. *Type the **$** and **&** in sets of three 10 times as shown below:*

$$$ &&& $$& &&$ $&$ &$& &&$ $$& $$$ &&&

Lesson 25: Numbers and Symbols: 5/% and 6/^ Keys

[Matthew 10:30, "And even the very hairs of your head are all numbered."]

Use your left index finger (F) for typing the **five (5)** and **percentage sign (%)**. Use your right index finger (J) for typing the **six (6)** and **caret (^)**. You use the right shift key for typing the percentage sign and the left shift key for typing the caret.

A. Type the **5** in sets of three 10 times as shown below:

555 555 555 555 555 555 555 555 555 555

B. Type the **6** in sets of three 10 times as shown below:

666 666 666 666 666 666 666 666 666 666

C. Type the **5** and **6** in sets of three 10 times as shown below:

555 666 565 656 556 665 556 665 555 666

D. Type the **%** in sets of three 10 time as shown below s:

%%% %%% %%% %%% %%% %%% %%% %%% %%% %%%

E. Type the **^** in sets of three 10 time as shown below s:

^^^ ^^^ ^^^ ^^^ ^^^ ^^^ ^^^ ^^^ ^^^ ^^^

F. Type the **%** and **^** in sets of three 10 times as shown below:

%%% ^^^ %%^ ^^% %%^ ^^% %^% ^%^ %%% ^^^

Lesson 26: Number Keypad: 4, 5, and 6 Keys

[Matthew 10:30, "And even the very hairs of your head are all numbered."]

*Allow your left hand to hover over the keyboard. You will need to use your left thumb to press the spacebar. Use your right index finger (J) for typing the **four (4)**, the right middle finger (K) for typing the **five (5)**, and the right ring finger for typing the **six (6)**. This is considered the home row for the numeric keypad.*

A. *Type the **4** in sets of three 10 times as shown below:*

444 444 444 444 444 444 444 444 444 444

B. *Type the **5** in sets of three 10 times as shown below:*

555 555 555 555 555 555 555 555 555 555

C. *Type the **6** in sets of three 10 times as shown below:*

666 666 666 666 666 666 666 666 666 666

D. *Type the **4**, **5** and **6** in sets of three 10 times as shown below:*

444 555 666 445 556 664 456 565 464 654

E. *Type the **4**, **5** and **6** in sets of three **as displayed** pressing **Enter** with your right pinky (on the numeric keypad) at the end of each line (typed as one column not two):*

444	546
555	465
666	564
456	645
645	664

Lesson 27: Number Keypad: 1, 2, and 3 Keys

[Matthew 10:30, "And even the very hairs of your head are all numbered."]

Allow your left hand to hover over the keyboard. You will need to use your left thumb to press the spacebar. Use your right index finger (J) for typing the **one (1)**, *the right middle finger (K) for typing the* **two (2)**, *and the right ring finger for typing the* **three (3)**.

A. *Type the **1** in sets of three 10 times as shown below:*

111 111 111 111 111 111 111 111 111 111

B. *Type the **2** in sets of three 10 times as shown below:*

222 222 222 222 222 222 222 222 222 222

C. *Type the **3** in sets of three 10 times as shown below:*

333 333 333 333 333 333 333 333 333 333

D. *Type the **1, 2** and **3** in sets of three 10 times as shown below:*

111 222 333 123 321 112 113 221 223 331

E. *Type the **1, 2** and **3** in sets of three **as displayed** pressing **Enter** with your right pinky (on the numeric keypad) at the end of each line (typed as one column not two):*

111	231
222	223
333	311
123	312
321	113

Lesson 28: Number Keypad: 7, 8, and 9 Keys

[Matthew 10:30, "And even the very hairs of your head are all numbered."]

*Allow your left hand to hover over the keyboard. You will need to use your left thumb to press the spacebar. Use your right index finger (J) for typing the **seven (7)**, the right middle finger (K) for typing the **eight (8)**, and the right ring finger for typing the **nine (9)**.*

A. *Type the **7** in sets of three 10 times as shown below:*

777 777 777 777 777 777 777 777 777 777

B *Type the **8** in sets of three 10 times as shown below:*

888 888 888 888 888 888 888 888 888 888

C. *Type the **9** in sets of three 10 times as shown below:*

999 999 999 999 999 999 999 999 999 999

D. *Type the **7**, **8** and **9** in sets of three 10 times as shown below:*

777 888 999 789 987 778 779 889 887 897

E. *Type the **7**, **8** and **9** in sets of three **as displayed** pressing **Enter** with your right pinky (on the numeric keypad) at the end of each line (typed as one column not two):*

777	798
888	897
999	978
789	787
987	989

Lesson 29: Number Keypad: 0 and . Keys and Review

[Matthew 10:30, "And even the very hairs of your head are all numbered."]

Allow your left hand to hover over the keyboard. You will need to use your left thumb to press the spacebar. Use your right index finger (J) for typing the **zero (0)**, and the right ring finger for typing the **decimal (.)**.

A. Type the **0** in sets of three 10 times as shown below:

000 000 000 000 000 000 000 000 000 000

B. Type the **.** in sets of three 10 times as shown below:

... ...

C. Type the **0** and **.** in sets of three 10 times as shown below:

000 ... 0.0 .0. 00. ..0 0.. ..0 000 ...

D. Type the **sets of numbers as displayed** pressing **Enter** with your right pinky (on the numeric keypad) at the end of each line (typed as one column not two):

456	124.44
123	672.0
789	640.579
12.4	1232.47
98.7	51.73

Lesson 30:   Horizontal and Vertical Centering

[Ezekiel 5:5, "This is what the Sovereign LORD says: This is Jerusalem,
which I have set in the center of the nations, with countries all around her."]

Use directions given by your instructor for formatting a document using both horizontal and vertical centering. Horizontal centering balances text between the left and right margins. Vertical centering balances text between the top and bottom margins.

*Using most word processors, horizontal centering is shown as an icon and also under Alignment, usually under the **Format** menu in the **Paragraph** menu option. There are two ways of centering horizontally. First, you may type the text and then select the text by highlighting with your mouse and selecting the centering icon. The second way is to select the centering icon and then type the text.*

*Vertical centering can also be done two ways. First, type the text, click on the **File** menu, select the **Page Setup** menu option, then the **Layout** tab. In the middle of this dialog box you will notice **Page** and **Vertical Alignment**. Select **Center** and press **OK**. Your text will move down automatically to adjust the page spacing.*

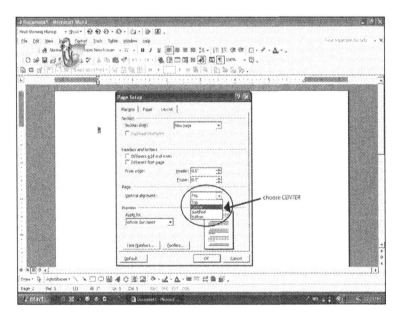

The following four Psalms, 100, 13, 63, and 19, are to be typed and centered horizontally and vertically.

Save each Psalm as the name of the Psalm, e.g. Psalm 63 or as directed by your instructor. Please note that God's name is capitalized (including His and Your).

Psalm 100

Shout for joy to the LORD, all the earth.
Worship the LORD with gladness;
come before Him with joyful songs.
Know that the LORD is God.
It is He who made us, and we are His;
we are His people, the sheep of His pasture.

Enter His gates with thanksgiving
and His courts with praise;
give thanks to Him and praise His name.
For the LORD is good and His love endures forever;
His faithfulness continues through all generations.

Psalm 13

How long, O LORD? Will You forget me forever?
How long will You hide Your face from me?
How long must I wrestle with my thoughts
and every day have sorrow in my heart?
How long will my enemy triumph over me?

Look on me and answer, O LORD my God.
Give light to my eyes, or I will sleep in death;
my enemy will say, "I have overcome him,"
and my foes will rejoice when I fall.

But I trust in Your unfailing love;
my heart rejoices in Your salvation.
I will sing to the LORD,
for He has been good to me.

Psalm 63

O God, You are my God,
earnestly I seek You;
my soul thirsts for You,
my body longs for You,
in a dry and weary land
where there is no water.

I have seen You in the sanctuary
and beheld Your power and Your glory.
Because Your love is better than life,
my lips will glorify You.
I will praise You as long as I live,
and in Your name I will lift up my hands.
My soul will be satisfied as with the richest of foods;
with singing lips my mouth will praise You.

On my bed I remember You;
I think of You through the watches of the night.
Because You are my help,
I sing in the shadow of Your wings.
My soul clings to You;
Your right hand upholds me.

They who seek my life will be destroyed;
they will go down to the depths of the earth.
They will be given over to the sword
and become food for jackals.

But the king will rejoice in God;
all who swear by God's name will praise Him,
while the mouths of liars will be silenced.

Psalm 19

The heavens declare the glory of God;
the skies proclaim the work of His hands.
Day after day they pour forth speech;
night after night they display knowledge.
There is no speech or language
where their voice is not heard.
Their voice goes out into all the earth,
their words to the ends of the world.
In the heavens He has pitched a tent for the sun,
which is like a bridegroom coming forth from His pavilion,
like a champion rejoicing to run His course.
It rises at one end of the heavens
and makes its circuit to the other;
nothing is hidden from its heat.
The law of the LORD is perfect,
reviving the soul.
The statutes of the LORD are trustworthy,
making wise the simple.
The precepts of the LORD are right,
giving joy to the heart.
The commands of the LORD are radiant,
giving light to the eyes.
The fear of the LORD is pure,
enduring forever.
The ordinances of the LORD are sure
and altogether righteous.
They are more precious than gold,
than much pure gold;
they are sweeter than honey,
than honey from the comb.
By them is Your servant warned;
in keeping them there is great reward.
Who can discern His errors?
Forgive my hidden faults.
Keep your servant also from willful sins;
may they not rule over me.
Then will I be blameless,
innocent of great transgression.
May the words of my mouth and the meditation of my heart
be pleasing in Your sight,
O Lord, my Rock and my Redeemer.

Lesson 31: Enumerated Lists

[Matthew 10:30, "And even the very hairs of your head are all numbered."]

*Enumeration is another word for numbering. Enumerating is a way of listing points for a topic. A list can use numbers, such as **1**, **2**, **3** or letters, such as **A**, **B**, **C**. The following exercise uses numbers.*

*Please note that once you start typing **1.** the word processor may start automatic numbering for you. The same is true for typing **A**. If you need to change the number or letter, double-click the letter or number and click on Restart Numbering or choose another format for your list. When double-line spacing, you may need to press **Enter** again for the blank line and then add the next enumerated item.*

*Lists featured alone on a page are normally centered vertically and contain two spaces from the letter or number to the text. If the text continues on subsequent lines; it is considered a **hanging indention** if it aligns under the previous text and not under the letter or number as shown by the exercise. Note the horizontal ruler settings for this exercise.*

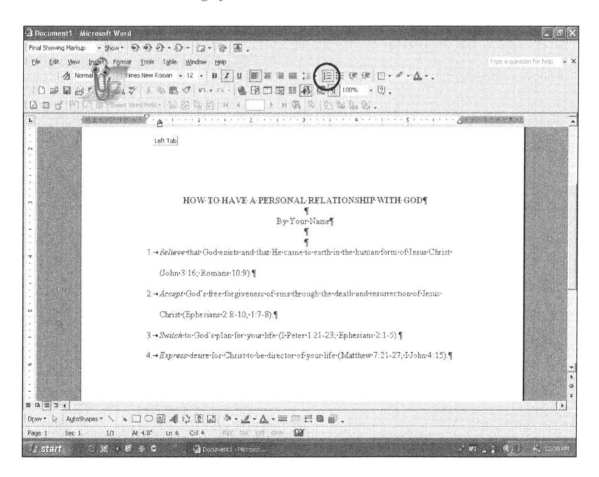

HOW TO HAVE A PERSONAL RELATIONSHIP WITH GOD

By Your Name

1. *Believe* that God exists and that He came to earth in the human form of Jesus Christ (John 3:16; Romans 10:9).

2. *Accept* God's free forgiveness of sins through the death and resurrection of Jesus Christ (Ephesians 2:8-10; 1:7-8).

3. *Switch* to God's plan for your life (I Peter 1:21-23; Ephesians 2:1-5).

4. *Express* desire for Christ to be director of your life (Matthew 7:21-27; I John 4:15).

Lesson 32: Tab Key

*Use your left pinky finger (A) for the **Tab** key. The **Tab** is normally used to indent paragraphs five spaces to the right by default. The Space Bar is not used before or after the **Tab**.*

__Tabs__ are also used to align text using custom markers known as left (default), right (where text begins on the right and moves towards the left), center (text is spread across), and decimal (numbers align at the decimal point). These are set by clicking on the horizontal ruler and manually placing the tabs in the desired locations. Or, this can be achieved by double clicking the ruler and using the dialog box by selecting the needed custom tab and typing in the location on the ruler or clearing previous tab settings.

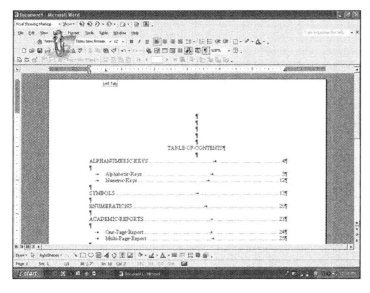

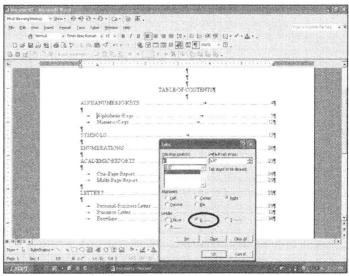

Creating a Table of Contents

In creating the following exercise, press **Enter six** times (or begin with a two inch top margin. After typing CONTENTS, press **Enter twice**. For each heading, use upper capital letters with double line spacing and initial caps for subheadings with single line spacing. **Dot leaders** (the dots that extend from the text to the page number) is done with a right tab and selecting the second leader from the Tabs dialog box.

The settings used are: .5 (left tab), 1 (subheading left tab), and 6 (right tab with dot leader 2 for page numbering).

CONTENTS

Lesson 33A: MLA Academic Reports

[Matthew 11:4, "Jesus answered and said unto them, Go and shew John again those things which ye do hear and see."]

The first two reports are formatted as MLA (Modern Language Association). The first one is a one-page report. The second is a multi-page report.

*Margins are set in the **File** menu under the **Page Setup** menu option and the **Margins** tab. Margins for an academic report are **1"** all around the page (top, bottom, and sides). Academic reports are double-spaced.*

*The **Heading** consists of the typed full name of the **student**, **teacher** name, **course** name, and a military-style **date** (day month year). These parts are all **double-spaced**. The reports in this book already have the 20__ ready for your input of the last two digits for the year. The title is centered horizontally and uses **initial caps** (capitalizing the first letter of important words similar to book titles).*

Lesson 33B: MLA Academic Reports

[Matthew 11:4, "Jesus answered and said unto them, Go and shew John again those things which ye do hear and see."]

The **second report** uses a **different heading** of the title in uppercase and bold and starts on line 12 (using your vertical ruler, use the **1** in the white area). This is followed by the byline (similar to newspapers or magazines). A triple space separates the byline and the heading which is in **bold**, **all caps**, and on its own line apart from the body text. The body text is **indented** (press **tab** once) five spaces. The **header** on the second page is the **last name** and **page numbering**— not shown on first page.

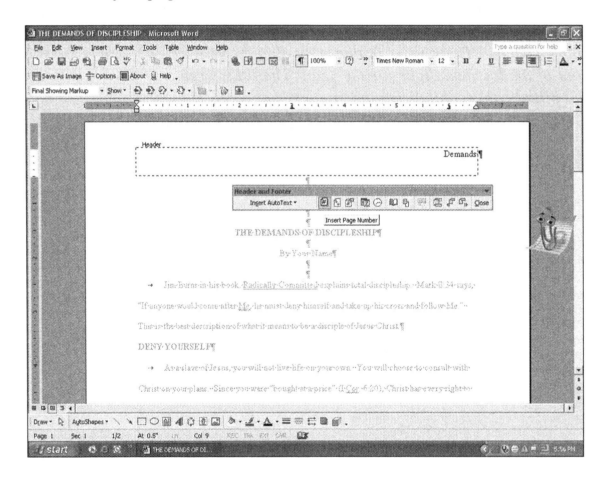

*Use the **View** menu and click on the **Header and Footer** menu option. A dashed textbox appears at the top of your page. Use the right alignment icon and type your **last name**. Then click on the **pound** symbol with a mouseover of **Insert Page Number**. To keep the header from appearing on the first page, click on the **book** icon with a mouseover of Page Setup and choose **Different first page** under Headers and Footers.*

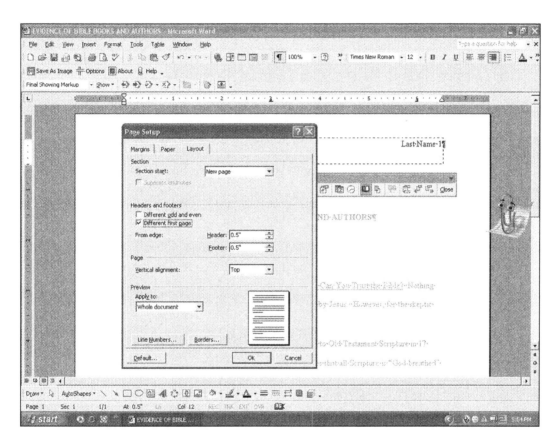

*   **Widow/orphan control** and **keep lines together** is used to keep a sentence from being split at the top and bottom of two pages or from wasting a few words of the sentence on a new page. Use the **Format** menu, click on the **Paragraph** menu option. Click on the **Line and Page Breaks** tab. Under **Pagination**, make sure check marks on shown in both the **Widow/Orphan control** box and in the **keep lines together** box, and press **OK**. Keep the major heading of **THE NEW TESTAMENT** with the text on the second page.*

*   *There is an **em dash** (a long hyphen) in the second report. Type **two hyphens** without spacing in between the text. Some word processors will translate this into a long dash automatically. If yours does not, then press **Enter** and backspace. The word processor will make the change.*

Your Name

Teacher Name

Keyboarding

1 October 20__

The Test of True Discipleship

Tony Campolo in his book, <u>You Can Make a Difference</u> tells the story of true discipleship. It's about a famous tightrope walker named Blondin. In the 1890s Blondin strung a tightrope across Niagara Falls, not only to demonstrate his skill but to challenge his audience.

Before ten thousand screaming people Blondin inched his way from the Canadian side of the falls to the United States side. When he got there the crowd began shouting his name: "Blondin! Blondin! Blondin! Blondin!"

Finally he raised his arms, quieted the crowd, and shouted to them, "I am Blondin! Do you believe in me?" The crowd shouted back, "We believe! We believe! We believe!"

He quieted them one more time, and then he said, "Who will be that person?" The crowd went dead. Nothing.

Finally, out of the crowd stepped one man. He climbed on Blondin's shoulders, and for the next three-and-a-half hours, Blondin inched his way back across the tightrope to the Canadian side of the falls.

The point of the story is blatantly clear: Ten thousand people stood there that day chanting, "We believe, we believe!" but only one person really believed. Believing is not just saying, "I accept the fact." Believing is giving your life over into the hands of the one in whom you say you believe.

EVIDENCE OF BIBLE BOOKS AND AUTHORS

By Your Name

THE OLD TESTAMENT

The following are excerpts from Ralph Muncaster's <u>Can You Trust the Bible?</u> Nothing more is needed than the confirmation of the Old Testament by Jesus. However, for the skeptic there is other evidence of God's inspiration.

- *The apostles confirmed it.* There are 212 references to Old Testament Scripture in 17 books of the New Testament. Paul specifically states that all Scripture is "God-breathed" (II Timothy 3:16).

- *Devout eyewitnesses confirmed it.* The Israelites were an intensely devout nation. A single error of prophecy caused the "prophet" to be stoned to death (and his work would not be regarded as Scripture). Most of the books of the Old Testament contain prophecy that was regarded as certain proof that something was of God (Deuteronomy 18:20-22, Isaiah 41:22-23).

- *Miraculous insight confirms it.* There is substantial evidence of God's authorship throughout the Old Testament, including miraculously fulfilled prophecy, scientific insights thousands of years before their discovery, concealed evidence throughout the Bible, and the precise, accurate account of creation.

THE NEW TESTAMENT

Again, the preauthorization and prophecies by Jesus for the New Testament are the most important evidence of its reliability. Yet other facts verify it as well:

♦ *Eyewitnesses confirmed it.* Imagine if today news reports said a person claiming to be God rose from the dead. Such a story would demand considerable confirmation before it would be taken seriously. Certainly a rumor would not survive strict scrutiny by eyewitnesses if it were false. If true, it might become an amazing classic. This describes the New Testament. The account was widely circulated while eyewitnesses were alive. Its circulation vastly exceeded that of any other document ever written. There are over 24,000 copies of the New Testament, 643 copies of Homer's Illiad, and seven copies of Pliny the Younger's Historical Works.

♦ *Death verified it.* Martyrdom for a *cause* is not new. Martyrdom for a known lie would be insane. All apostles certainly *knew* the truth and died violent deaths (except John) to verify the account.

♦ *The early church believed it.* The Gospels and letters were considered Scripture—equal to the Old Testament.

Lesson 34: APA Academic Reports

[Matthew 11:4, "Jesus answered and said unto them, Go and shew John again those things which ye do hear and see."]

*The next report is a three-page report that uses APA formatting. APA stands for American Psychological Association. You will need to insert a header with a **shortened title** and **page numbering** (not shown on the first page of reports). Use the **View** menu and click on the **Header and Footer** menu option. A dashed textbox appears at the top of your page. Use the right alignment icon and type your **shortened title**. Then click on the **pound** symbol with a mouseover of **Insert Page Number**. To keep the header from appearing on the first page, click on the **book** icon with a mouseover of Page Setup and choose **Different first page** under Headers and Footers.*

*APA reports are similar to the MLA multi-page reports. The margins are still 1" all around except for the first page where text begins on line 12. Then type the **title** in **all caps** followed by a double-space, then the **byline** and a triple-space to the body. The body uses double-spacing.*

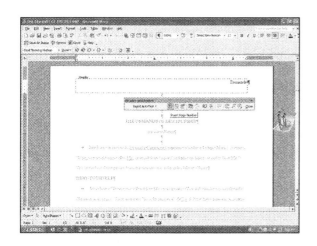

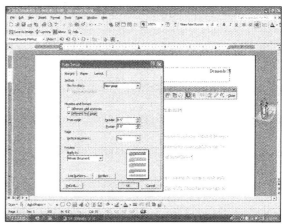

THE DEMANDS OF DISCIPLESHIP

By Your Name

Jim Burns in his book, <u>Radically Committed</u> explains total discipleship. Mark 8:34 says, "If anyone would come after Me, he must deny himself and take up his cross and follow Me." This is the best description of what it means to be a disciple of Jesus Christ.

DENY YOURSELF

As a slave of Jesus, you will not live life on your own. You will choose to consult with Christ on your plans. Since you were "bought at a price" (I Cor. 6:20), Christ has every right to make demands on your life. You're *His* now.

If you choose to come after Christ, you are choosing to balk at our society's prevailing attitudes and philosophy. You have to count the cost of self-denial if you choose to team up with Jesus. Are you willing to make the cause of Christ your overwhelming first love?

TAKE UP YOUR CROSS

To take up your cross means to sacrifice. It means to have the kind of courage displayed by a Christian named Telemachus, in the fourth century. He was a monk who had spent most of his life in study and prayer. One day he felt that the Lord wanted him to go to Rome. He had no idea why he should go there, and he was terrified at the thought. But as he prayed, God's directive became clear. He arrived in Rome during a holiday festival when the Romans defeated the Goths.

He still did not understand why God had brought him there but let the crowds guide him. They all went into the Coliseum, where the gladiator contests were to be staged. He could hear the cries of the animals in their cages beneath the floor of the great arena and the clamor of the contestants preparing to do battle.

The gladiators marched into the arena, saluted the emperor, and shouted, "We who are about to die salute thee." Telemachus shuddered. He had never heard of these games before, but he had an idea of the awful violence. Human lives were offered for entertainment. As the monk realized what was going to happen, he realized he could not sit still and watch such savagery. He jumped to the top of the wall and cried, "In the name of Christ, forbear!"

Since no one paid attention to him, he went to the floor of the arena. Again, he shouted, "In the name of Christ, forbear!" His movement blocked the vision of one of the gladiators which infuriated the crowd. They screamed, "Run him through!" The gladiator raised his sword and with a flash of steel struck Telemachus, slashing down across his chest and into his stomach. The monk gasped once more, "In the name of Christ, forbear!"

Then a strange thing occurred. As the gladiators and crowd focused on his still form, the arena grew deathly quiet. In the silence, someone in the top tier of the arena got up and walked out. Another followed. All over the arena, spectators began to leave, until the huge stadium was emptied. It became the last gladiatorial contest ever held there.

For Telemachus, taking up the cross meant to die for the cause. For most of us it doesn't mean a martyr's death as much as it means standing up for what is right, and for what honors God. Sometimes it seems that it may be easier to stand in front of the Roman Coliseum than to stand up for what is right in our own home, community, or school. God puts a cause in

everyone's heart. Your cross may be drunk driving, poverty, abortion, war, refugees, or hundred of other important causes. As you come after Christ, are you willing to take up His cross and change the world?

FOLLOW ME

Jesus said simply, "Follow Me." Who are you following? Are you following after your own decisions, or can you say you are a follower of Jesus Christ? Are you willing to *go* wherever Jesus wants you to go? Are you willing to *be* whatever Jesus wants you to be? To follow Christ means to release your life into His hands and trust that the God Who created the universe can do a better job of running your life than you can.

Deep down, most people don't want a tame, humdrum, sheltered monotony of faith. They are seeking a thrilling adventure of radical discipleship. To become a disciple means to learn of Jesus, to follow His teaching, and frankly, imitate His life to the best of your ability. When you really follow you become not only His servant but His slave. You were bought with a very high price—God hung on a cross. When you come after Jesus your life becomes His life. Paul said in Galatians 2:20, "I have been crucified with Christ and I no longer live, but Christ lives in me. The life I live in the body, I live by faith in the Son of God, Who loved me and gave Himself for me."

Lesson 35A: Cover Page

Multi-page reports are the most common for classes. Usually a cover page is required for the report.

The MLA format for the first cover page shown includes a header with the student's last name and one space before the page number.

*Press **Enter** 10 times and type the title of the report using initial caps (capitalizing only the important words). Press **Enter** five times and type your name. Press **Enter** five more times and type the name of the class, the teacher's name, and the due date (written out). Some schools also include the school name after the student name. Create one of these two cover pages as instructed.*

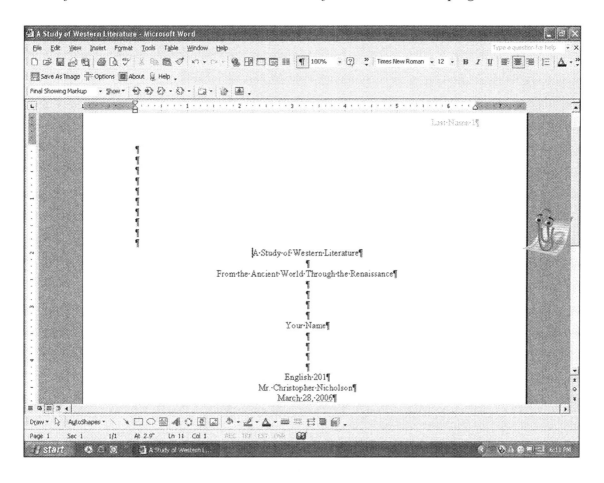

Lesson 35B: APA Cover Page

The APA format uses a shortened version of the title, five spaces, and then the page number. This text will use the one space instead of the five (which is the most common).

*Press **Enter** 10 times and type the title of the report using initial caps (capitalizing only the important words). Press **Enter** five times and type your name. Press **Enter** five more times and type the name of the class, the teacher's name, and the due date (written out). Some schools also include the school name after the student name. Create one of these two cover pages as instructed.*

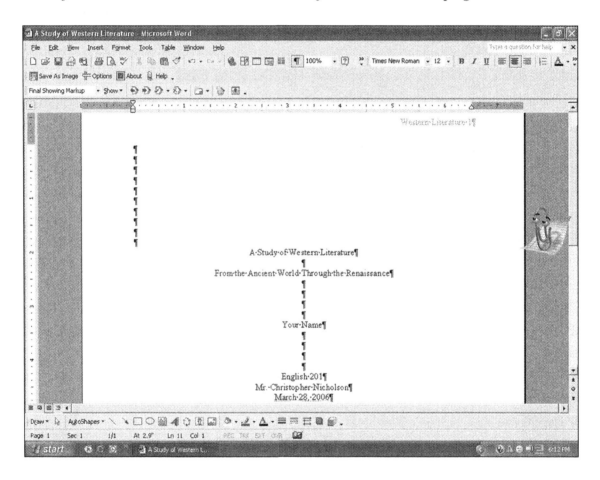

Lesson 36: Works Cited

[John 7:28b, "Yes you know Me, and you know where I am from.
I am not here on My own, but He Who sent Me is true…"]

*Works Cited is normally required for verification of sources cited in an MLA report. This is the last page of a report. Each item is double-spaced and uses the same margins as the report. The title of Works Cited is **centered**. The citations are listed in alphabetical order by the author's last name. If the name is unknown, then the title is used alphabetically. Additional lines are formatted using a hanging indention.*

*The following items are used in the Works Cited: last name of author, first name, additional authors (for several, **et. al.** is used), the title of the work, the publisher's city and then the publisher name, the year of publication, and applicable page numbers.*

Type the Works Cited as shown below. Use the same header as the report.

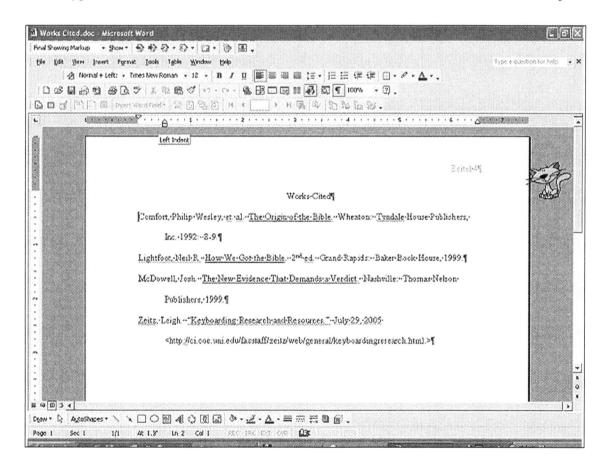

Lesson 37: Bibliography

[John 7:28b, "Yes you know Me, and you know where I am from.
I am not here on My own, but He Who sent Me is true…"]

A ***bibliography*** *is normally required for verification of sources cited in an APA report. This is the last page of a report. Each item is double-spaced and uses the same margins as the report. The title of Bibliography is **centered** and in **bold**. It starts on **line 12**. The citations are listed in alphabetical order by the author's last name. If the name is unknown, then the title is used alphabetically. Additional lines are formatted using a hanging indention.*

*The following items are used in the Bibliography: last name of author, first name, additional authors (for several, **et. al.** is used), the year of publication, the title of the work, the publisher's city and then the publisher name, and applicable page numbers. Each item is single-spaced with a blank line in between citations. Type the Bibliography as shown below.*

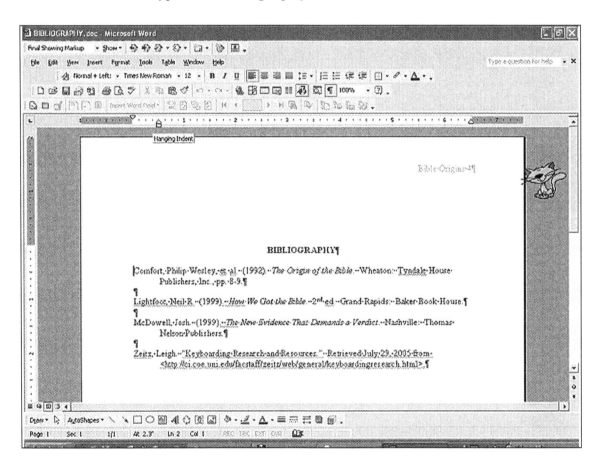

Lesson 38:   Personal-Business Letters

[Luke 1:3, "It seemed good to me also, having had perfect understanding of all things from the very first, to write unto thee in order, most excellent Theophilus,"]

A personal-business letter is written from an individual to a business. These are more formal than the typical personal letters written to friends or relatives. Examples include writing a letter to a company commending their service or complaining about a missing part from an order.

The parts and line spacing of a personal-business letter are:

Dateline, *press* **Enter** *four times.*

Inside address *(name and address of receiver), press* **Enter** *twice but use single-line spacing. Notice that the state abbreviation is capitalized and street names are spelled out (e.g. Lane, Street, Road, Boulevard), but directions are not.*

Salutation, *press* **Enter** *twice.*

Body, *press* **Enter** *twice between paragraphs but use single-line spacing within each paragraph.*

Complimentary closing, *press* **Enter** *four times to leave room for the*

Writer's Signature, *(signed after printing) and*

Writer's Identification *(name and address of writer), use single-line spacing.*

Older styles of this letter format included the writer's address before the dateline instead of after the writer's name.

Margins for letters are **1"** *top and bottom,* **1.25"** *sides. After typing the letter,* **center** *the letter* **vertically** *but* **not horizontally.**

The format for the four letters is **block style. Nothing is indented.**

When using newer word processors, a pink dotted line may appear under an address or the dateline. This is called a smart tag. It will not print. It is for additional tasks such as scheduling an event or mapping an address.

November 2, 2006

Mr. Randy Washington
Topper, Inc.
3709 W. California Street
Garland, TX 75042

Dear Mr. Washington:

Topper, Inc. is the number one company in the frozen pizza toppings industry. I would like to apply for the part-time customer service position you advertised in the Dallas Morning News.

Although my work background is slim, I think I can offer Topper, Inc. a strong desire to excel in customer service based upon my experience as a volunteer with Key Club. Our community service projects included providing meals for the downtown homeless shelter on a weekly basis, asking for donations from local businesses to provide clothing and medical care for the children's hospital, and Habitat for Humanity.

Your requirements included a high school diploma and typing 40 wpm. I will be graduating from Dallas Christian Academy in May 2007. My business courses include keyboarding and computer applications. My typing speed is currently 65 wpm.

I would like to discuss this position with you and will be happy to come in for an interview at your convenience. Please call me during the day at 972-555-1234 between 3 p.m. and 7 p.m. Thank you for your time and consideration.

Sincerely,

Student Name
10105 Mary Kay Lane
Dallas, TX 75231

April 22, 2006

Ms. Lea Kyle, General Manager
Universal Trains
P. O. Box 1204
Madison, WI 53703-1204

Dear Ms. Kyle:

I was recently in Madison for a church convention as a volunteer youth worker and visited the Universal Trains store. The Lionel Train collection was enjoyable. Your displays are very realistic. The mountain pass of Oregon hit by recent wildfires was spectacular—it really looked like a different planet with the charred trees and hardened lava. The Christmas trains winding around a Dicken's village was also beautiful with the colored lights in the trees and buildings.

The modeling department of Universal Trains offers tours for groups of five or more on Saturdays only with discounts on groups of 20 or more. My church youth group is interested in bringing 20 fifth-graders to your shop. The students have requested to view where the trains and accessories are first created for public display. We would like to arrive on Saturday, May 27, 2006 for a tour at the discounted rate of $5 per student.

If this is possible, please call me at 414-423-1234 during the hours of 9 a.m. until 5 p.m. Thank you for your time.

Sincerely yours,

Student Name
C/O Pleasant Road Baptist Church
W. 160 S. 7255 Avery Drive
Milwaukee, WI 53215

February 10, 2006

Dr. Neelu Patel, Head Pharmacy Technician
Health First Cape Canaveral Hospital
701 W. Cocoa Beach Causeway
Cocoa Beach, FL 32931

Dear Dr. Patel:

Our class is studying the results of chlorine in drinking water. We read your interesting essay from the Internet showing the risks associated with too much chlorine versus filtering devices used by municipal water treatment facilities and wanted to know more.

We understand that your hospital has researched ocean water and chemicals along with the city water supply and that you have been active in government funding for this research. Our local television stations have monitored your progress in getting this funding.

Since this is a class project, we would like some suggestions that we could use to inform our own government officials to make sure our drinking water is safe. Any additional materials in this would be greatly appreciated.

Thank you for your assistance. Any materials you can offer our class can be sent to our science teacher, Mrs. Laura Jennings at the address listed below.

Sincerely yours,

Student Name
Pensacola Christian High School
3708 Melissa Lane
Pensacola, FL 32501

September 26, 2006

Mr. Robert Lawler, Region 6 Contest Coordinator
Business Professionals of America Regional Office
P. O. Box 82199-4359
Tulsa, OK 74171-4359

Dear Mr. Lawler:

The computer applications class at Lake Country Academy is interested in attending the next Business Professionals of America competition in March 2007. We have participated in similar contests for Future Business Leaders of America. The only difference is that this contest will be a weeklong competition in Arkansas next spring versus a one-day event.

Our school will use the van which seats 16 students and two chaperones. Is there a schedule of events for students to review with their parents? We want to enjoy as much as we can yet not be there for the entire week since this will be the week of our spring break.

What housing will be available for the competition? Will the students be able to walk around the campus while not in session? Will there be transportation from the housing to the campus?

Is food covered by the housing or are there arrangements inside the building? If not, are there inexpensive restaurants close to the housing and/or campus?

When the contests are completed, what is available for entertainment for the students?

We appreciate answers to these questions before we register for the competition and for our fundraising projects.

Cordially yours,

Student Name
Lake Country Academy
115115 Jeffrey Blvd.
Broken Arrow, OK 74012

Lesson 39: Business Letters

(Luke 1:3, "It seemed good to me also, having had perfect understanding of all things from the very first, to write unto thee in order, most excellent Theophilus,")

The business letter is written by an employee of a business and is sent to either another business, or to an individual. This includes non-profit organizations and schools. The previous letters were from students—not considered business letters. Business letter parts are the same as the personal-business letter parts.

Business letters are typed on company stationery, which is preprinted with the company name, address, phone number, website, e-mail address, and sometimes a logo.

Instead of typing the writer's address, the writer's title is used. A title could be Administrative Assistant or Customer Service Manager. Also, a new part is introduced, the typist's initials, also known as the reference initials; which is double-spaced after the writer's title. There are several ways for the typist to use this.

*The current way, is to type the writer's uppercase initials, a colon, and then the typist's lowercase initials without any spacing (e.g. **LB:bh**). Previously secretaries (or administrative assistants), would type the writer's uppercase initials, a forward slash, and then the typist's lowercase initials without any spacing (e.g. LB/bh). This text will use the first method described. An "xx" will be used in the text for the student to place their initials.*

*The **first two** letters are **block style**—no indenting just as the personal-business letter is formatted. The **last two** letters will use a **modified-block** style with indented paragraphs. Modified block style means that the dateline, complimentary closing, writer's name and title will be **tabbed at the center** of the letter. Typically this is a tab setting of **2.5" or 3.0"** based upon the size of the date. For longer dates, such as December 14, 2006, use the tab setting of 2.5". For shorter dates, such as May 3, 2006, use the tab setting of 3.0".*

*The last letter is a **two-page** letter with the header showing the second page information of recipient, page number, and date. Enclosure notation lets the recipient know to expect other items with the letter. Carbon copy (cc) is followed by two spaces and the name of the person getting the copy.*

August 29, 2006

Mrs. Ginger Carson
3830 Hensley Drive
Fort Worth, TX 76134

Dear Mrs. Carson:

Reference:	Insured:	Carson
	Claimant:	Elisa Green
	Policy No.:	TXS 00293842
	Claim No.:	94820
	Loss Date:	August 15, 2006

We have completed our investigation into this accident.

Based upon our investigation, the policy for you with our company expired on August 10, 2006 and was not in effect at the time of this accident. Accordingly, we can find no coverage that would apply to this accident and will be unable to honor your claim.

If you have any additional information that might change our findings, please forward it to the undersigned immediately.

Sincerely,

Caroline Dennis
Claims Adjuster

CD:xx
cc: Elisa Green

November 2, 2006

Rev. Ken Dable
Oklahoma City Bible Church
4003 Beverly Boulevard
Oklahoma City, OK 73106

Dear Rev. Dable:

Thank you for your generous contribution of $5,000 to Concerned Christians of Oklahoma, the state's largest public policy organization for Christians. In these difficult times, the uplifting prayers and generous support from loyal members like you sustain us.

We are living in perilous times, and the moral values you and I share are becoming more endangered with each passing day. Many citizens in Oklahoma feel that their values are not being upheld in our court system. With your contribution, we are making changes to keep our Christian morals in our state laws.

At the writing of this letter, our representatives from Concerned Christians of Oklahoma are lobbying for the sanctity of life in our state courts. We are also fighting for the sacred institution of marriage.

Thank you once again for your support; good and faithful servants like you are not only the backbone of our organization, but of America itself. Enclosed is the receipt for your donation.

Warm regards,

Sue Marshall
Oklahoma City Chapter President

SM:xx
Enclosure

October 11, 2006

Ms. Christine Shirley
254 W. 6th Street
Austin, TX 78701

Dear Ms. Shirley:

Thank you for your recent order from our 2006 fall catalog. The brown bear coffee table and matching end table you ordered is of the highest quality. It is made in Red River, New Mexico by a master woodcarver.

Currently, the coffee table is on backorder from Red River due to the increase in demand for these unique pieces. We expect to have the table delivered to you within the next three weeks.

We apologize for any inconvenience this may have caused you and would like to offer you a $50 gift certificate for your next order. The gift certificate is enclosed. We have also included samples from our country store of homemade peanut brittle and honey.

Sincerely,

Madeline Edwards, Manager
Bear Country Furnishings Department

ML:xx
Enclosures (3)
cc: Jacob Chadwick, Shipping

January 23, 2006

Mr. Curtis Mahan
4377 Sarah Drive
Little Rock, AR 72202

Dear Mr. Mahan:

We are in receipt of, and hereby acknowledge, your medical claim for workman's compensation benefits for Zenith Enterprises for the injury incurred in the mail room on January 11, 2006.

While the details of your workman's compensation benefits are found in your contract, including any conditions or exclusions, the following items should be covered: reasonable expenses incurred for necessary medical services and lost wages.

Please assist us in considering your claim for benefits by providing us with the following items, statements, and forms:

1. Contact us so that we may discuss this injury with you
2. Please complete and return the company's Full Accident Detail Report
3. Complete and return the Authorization to Provide Coverage form
4. Provide us with copies of all medical bills and records
5. Provide us with the names, addresses, and phone numbers for all medical providers associated with this injury
6. Have your physician or the company physician complete and return the attached Attending Physician Report
7. Have your physician complete and return the attached Able to Return to Work form when you are released from medical care
8. If you are making a claim for loss of income, provide us with the name of your supervisor and department number
9. Have your supervisor complete and return the enclosed Wage and Salary Verification form
10. Please provide copies of all prescription receipts, along with the medication name, associated with this injury
11. Please provide copies of any explanation of benefits you have received from the health insurer as a result of this accident

Mr. Curtis Mahan
January 23, 2006
Page 2

As we continue to investigate, it may become necessary for us to request additional information in order to secure final documentation of your injury sustained at Zenith. We are concerned for your condition and want to make sure that you will be able to return to work when you are fully recovered.

Please contact me should you have any further questions or concerns regarding this claim. Thank you in advance for your patience and cooperation.

Sincerely,

Joyce Scheffler
Claim Representative

JS:xx
Enclosures (5)
cc: Judith Leroy

Lesson 40:   Envelopes

[Job 7:18b, "that You examine him every morning and test him every moment?"]

Letters meant to be mailed need an envelope. There are two main types of envelopes: standard (for business use) and stationery (for personal use). Letters are normally printed on 8.5" x 11" paper. The standard envelope, also called the No. 10 envelope because it measures 9 ½" x 4 ⅛" and the smaller one is called the No. 6 envelope due to its measurements of 3 ⅝" x 6 ½".

Envelopes are manually fed into the printer. Sometimes there is a special tray for envelope size adjustments. Since most businesses use preprinted letterhead; they also used preprinted envelopes. In these exercises, you will only need to use the recipient's delivery address (inside address).

Place your cursor by the inside address in the letter. Choose the Tools menu. Click on Letters and Mailings and choose the Envelopes and Labels dialog box.

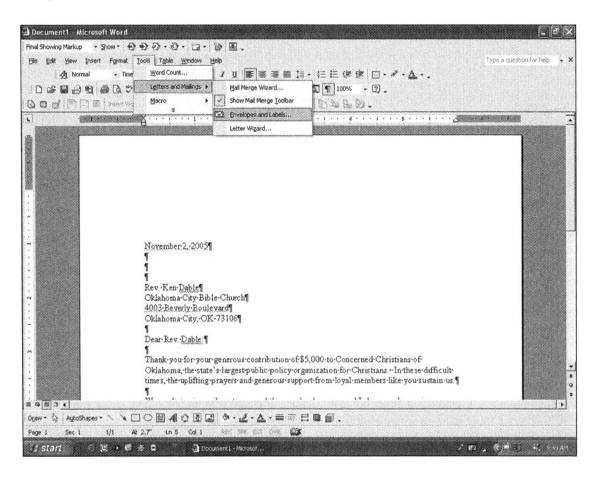

Click on Omit for the Return Address and press Add to Document for the Delivery Address. The second picture shows the end result.

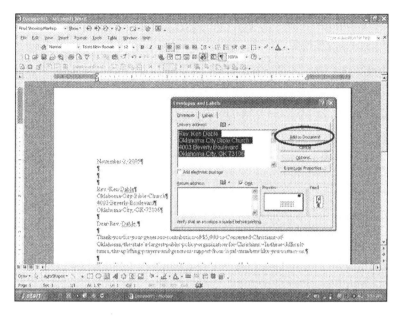

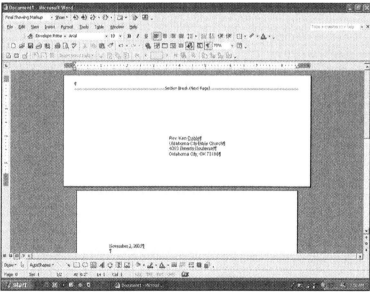

Envelopes Exercise

Create envelopes for four of the letters typed in the previous sections. Don't forget to omit the return address.

Lesson 41: Proofreader's Marks

[Psalm 11:4b, "He observes the sons of men; His eyes examine them."]

*Editors use special handwritten marks as they are checking for errors. These marks are then used by journalists to make the appropriate changes. Spell check and grammar check features in software are not always accurate. An example of this is the word **to**. There are different variations with different meanings: to, too, two, and 2. That is why work is checked carefully.*

Proofreader's Mark	Example	Correction
Insert word/letter	How strong is my faih?	How strong is my faith?
Delete word/letter	We will study the Bible	We will study the Bible tomorrow.
Insert a period	God examines man's ways	God examines man's ways.
Insert a comma or semicolon	Get wisdom get understanding	Get wisdom, get understanding;
Change word	Read the words carefully.	Read the text carefully.
Insert space	That's the wrongone!	That's the wrong one!
Delete space	Fill in the application completely.	Fill in the application completely.
Lowercase	Jesus Loves you!	Jesus loves you!
Capitalize	god is holy.	God is holy.
Move as shown	can see God's hand in their Students lives.	Students can see God's hand in their lives.
Start new paragraph	How are you? I am doing well.	How are you? I am doing well.
Don't make change (stet)	I'm so glad Jesus set me free!	I'm so glad Jesus set me free!

Proofreader's Mark	Example	Correction
Transpose (rearrange)	Jesus the is light of the world.	Jesus is the light of the world.
Apply bold	Shout for joy!	Shout for **joy**!
Apply italics *ital*	English students will be reading the article, "Truth or Fiction".	English students will be reading the article, *"Truth or Fiction"*.
Apply underline *u/l*	The library has <u>Time</u> magazine for students.	The library has <u>Time</u> magazine for students.
Spell out (numbers or direction)	The 1st church is on Main St.	The first church is on Main Street.
Move text to the right	19456.3 +9028.5	19456.3 +9028.5
Move text to the left	I appreciated your gift.	I appreciated your gift.
Apply single spacing ss	Take every thought captive.	Take every thought captive.
Apply double spacing ds	This report will examine How effective time management can be.	This report will examine how effective time management can be.

Proofreader's Marks Exercise

Using the chart, write five sentences with errors and proofreader's marks. Have another student correct the sentences.

Lesson 42: Timed Writings (Timings)

[Job 7:18, "that You examine him every morning and test him every moment?"]

Typing speed is determined by characters (letter, number, symbol, or space). For every five characters one typed word is created. Beginning timings offer three and four letter words with a space between the words. Longer words may be counted as more than one typed word. The word **decoration** *is longer than the word* **was***. In this case,* **decoration** *counts as two typed words and* **was** *is not a complete typed word.*

Typed words are translated into a measurement called gross words a minute (gwam) or words per minute (wpm). Any number of errors in a word counts as one error. After subtracting errors, the result is the net words per minute (nwpm). Each line shows how many words have been typed in one minute. Add the numbers together for each line completed and then determine unfinished lines by counting out each five characters as one typed word.

Lesson 6, ex. H
TIMING: *Type the following lines for one minute. Repeat if time permits. Press* **Enter** *once after each line.*

dad dad lad lad had had   5 words typed for the first line
  ‾‾‾‾‾‾‾‾‾‾‾‾‾‾‾‾‾‾‾‾‾
   1   2   3   4   5

gag gag sad sad fad fad   5 words typed for the second line
  ‾‾‾‾‾‾‾‾‾‾‾‾‾‾‾‾‾‾‾‾‾
   1   2   3   4   5

Lesson 8, ex. F
TIMING: *Type the following lines for one minute. Repeat if time permits. Press* **Enter** *once after each line.*

said said dark dark like like   6
  ‾‾‾‾‾‾‾‾‾‾‾‾‾‾‾‾‾‾‾‾‾‾‾‾
   1   2   3   4   5   6

deal deal hear hear feel feel   6
  ‾‾‾‾‾‾‾‾‾‾‾‾‾‾‾‾‾‾‾‾‾‾‾‾
   1   2   3   4   5   6

Lesson 10, ex. F
TIMING: *Type the following lines for one minute. Repeat if time permits. Press* **Enter** *once after each line.*

your your good good life life   6
——————————————————
  1   2   3   4   5   6

true true gate gate will will   6
——————————————————
  1   2   3   4   5   6

Lesson 12, ex. H
TIMING: *Type the following lines for one minute. Repeat if time permits. Press* **Enter** *once after each line.*

hope hope page page half half   6
——————————————————
  1   2   3   4   5   6

yoke yoke loud loud grade grade   6
——————————————————
  1   2   3   4   5   6

Lesson 14, ex. F
TIMING: *Type the following lines for one minute. Repeat if time permits. Press* **Enter** *once after each line.*

gift gift seen seen warm warm   6
——————————————————
  1   2   3   4   5   6

mail mail vets vets quit quit   6
——————————————————
  1   2   3   4   5   6

Lesson 16, ex. F
TIMING: *Type the following lines for one minute. Repeat if time permits. Press* **Enter** *once after each line.*

exam exam root root slab slab   6
——————————————————
  1   2   3   4   5   6

oxen oxen cave cave name name   6
——————————————————
  1   2   3   4   5   6

Lesson 18, ex. E, Psalm 117

TIMING: *Type the following lines for two, three or five minutes. Repeat if time permits. Press **Enter** once after each line. For scoring, divide the nwpm by the time used. For example, 30 nwpm typed in three minutes equals 10 npwm.*

Praise the LORD, all you   4

   1   2   3   4   5

nations; Extol Him, all you peoples.   7

   1   2   3   4   5   6   7

For great is His love toward us, and   7

   1   2   3   4   5   6   7

the faithfulness of the LORD endures forever.   9

   1   2   3   4   5   6   7   8   9

Praise the LORD.   3

   1   2   3

Lesson 20, ex. G, Psalm 15

TIMING: *Same directions as Lesson 18.*

LORD, who may dwell   4
in Your sanctuary? Who   4
may live on Your holy hill?   5
He whose walk is blameless   5
and who does what is   4
righteous, who speaks the   5
truth from his heart   4
and has no slander on his   5
tongue, who does his neighbor   6
no wrong and casts no slur   5
on his fellowman, who despises   6
a vile man but honors those who fear the   8
LORD, who keeps oath even when   6
it hurts, who lends his money   6
without usury and does not accept a bribe against   10
the innocent. He who does these things   8
will never be shaken.   4

   1   2   3   4   5   6   7   8   9   10

Lesson 22, ex. G, Psalm 1
TIMING: Same directions as Lesson 18.

Blessed is the man who does not walk in	8
the counsel of the wicked or stand in the	8
way of sinners or sit in the seat of mockers.	9
But his delight is in the law of the LORD, and	9
on His law he meditates day and night. He	8
is like a tree planted by streams of water,	8
which yields its fruit in season and whose	8
leaf does not wither. Whatever he does	8
prospers. Not so the wicked! They are	8
like chaff that the wind blows away.	7
Therefore the wicked will not stand	7
in the Judgment, nor sinners in the	7
assembly of the righteous.	5
For the LORD watches over the way of	7
the righteous, but the way of the wicked	8
will perish.	2

1	2	3	4	5	6	7	8	9	10

Lesson 24, ex. G, Psalm 23
TIMING: Same directions as Lesson 18.

The LORD is my shepherd, I shall not be	8
in want. He makes me lie down	6
in green pastures, He leads me	6
beside quiet waters, He restores my	7
soul. He guides me in paths of	6
righteousness for His name's sake. Even though I	10
walk through the valley of the shadow of	8
death, I will fear no evil, for You are with	9
me; Your rod and Your staff, they comfort me.	9
You prepare a table before me in the presence	9
of my enemies. You anoint my head with oil;	9
my cup overflows. Surely goodness and love will follow	11
me all the days of my life, and I will dwell in the	10
house of the LORD forever.	5

1	2	3	4	5	6	7	8	9	10	11	12

Lesson 26, ex. F, Psalm 26
TIMING: Same directions as Lesson 18.

Vindicate me, O LORD, for I	5
have led a blameless life; I have trusted in	9
the LORD without wavering. Test me, O LORD,	9
and try me, examine my heart and my mind; for Your love	11
is ever before me, and I walk continually in your truth. I do not sit	14
with deceitful men, nor do I consort with hypocrites; I abhor the	13
assembly of evildoers and refuse to sit with the wicked. I	12
wash my hands in innocence, and go about Your altar, O LORD,	12
proclaiming aloud Your praise and telling of	9
all Your wonderful deeds. I love the house where You live,	12
O LORD, the place where Your glory dwells. Do not take away	12
my soul along with sinners, my life with bloodthirsty men,	12
in whose hands are wicked schemes, whose right hands are full of	13
bribes. But I lead a blameless life; redeem me and be merciful to me.	14
My feet stand on level ground; in the great assembly I	11
will praise the LORD.	4

1   2   3   4   5   6   7   8   9   10   11   12   13   14

Lesson 28, ex. E, Psalm 84
TIMING: Same directions as Lesson 18.

How lovely is your dwelling place, O LORD Almighty!	10
My soul yearns, even faints, for the courts of the LORD;	11
my heart and my flesh cry out for the living	9
God. Even the sparrow has found a home, and	9
the swallow a nest for herself, where she may have her young;	12
a place near Your altar, O LORD Almighty, my King	10
and my God, blessed are those who dwell in Your house;	11
they are ever praising You. Blessed are those whose strength is	13
in You, who have set their hearts on pilgrimage. As they pass through	14
the Valley of Baca, they make it a place of spring; the autumn rains also cover	16
it with pools. They go from strength to strength, till each	12
appears before God in Zion. Hear my prayer, O LORD God Almighty;	13
listen to me, O God of Jacob; Look upon our shield, O God; look with	13
favor on Your anointed one. Better is one day in Your	11
courts than a thousand elsewhere; I would rather be a doorkeeper in the house of	16
my God than dwell in the tents of the wicked.	9
For the LORD God is a sun and shield; the LORD bestows favor	12
and honor; no good thing does	6
He withhold from those whose walk is blameless. O	10
LORD Almighty, blessed is the man who trusts in You.	10

1   2   3   4   5   6   7   8   9   10   11   12   13   14   15   16   17

Keyboarding Timed Writing Scale

FIRST/FOURTH SIX WEEKS' ONE-TWO MINUTE SPEEDS

	SPEED	35+	32-34	29-31	26-28	23-25	20-22	17-19	14-16	11-13	8-10
ERRORS											
0-12	GRADE	100	95	90	85	80	75	70	65	60	50

SECOND/FIFTH SIX WEEKS' TWO-THREE MINUTE SPEEDS

	SPEED	36+	33-35	30-32	27-29	24-26	21-23	18-20	15-17	12-14	9-11
ERRORS											
0-2	GRADE	100	94	92	90	88	86	84	82	80	78
3-5		93	87	85	83	81	79	77	75	73	71
6-7		86	80	78	76	74	72	70	68	66	64
8-10		79	73	71	69	67	65	63	61	59	57
11-12		72	66	64	62	60	58	56	54	52	50

THIRD/SIXTH SIX WEEKS' FIVE MINUTE SPEEDS

	SPEED	39+	36-39	33-35	30-32	27-29	24-26	21-23	18-20	15-17	12-14
ERRORS											
0-2	GRADE	100	94	92	90	88	86	84	82	80	78
3-5		93	87	85	83	81	79	77	75	73	71
6-7		86	80	78	76	74	72	70	68	66	64
8-10		79	73	71	69	67	65	63	61	59	57
11-12		72	66	64	62	60	58	56	54	52	50

Index

978-0-595-38319-1
0-595-38319-X